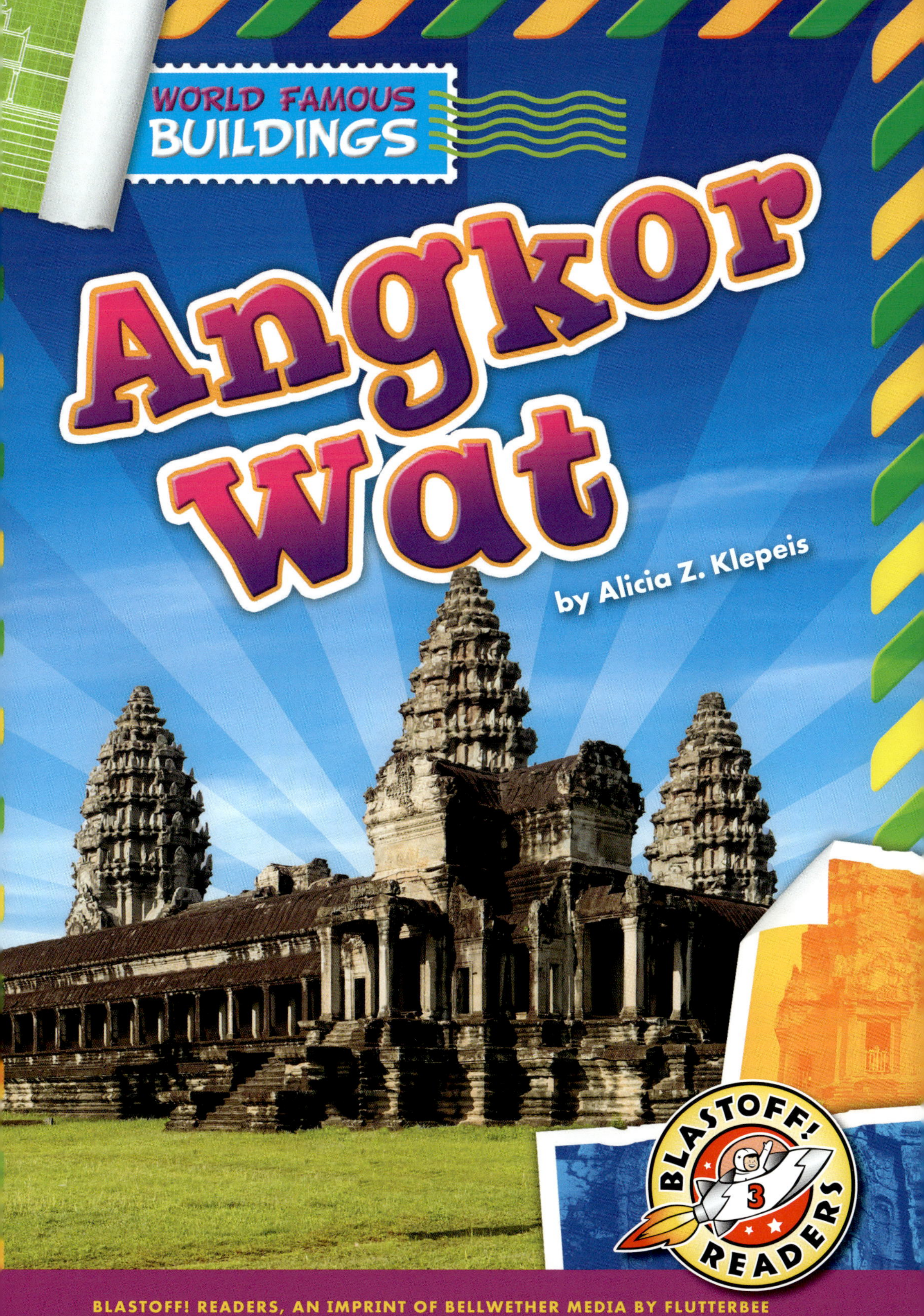

BLASTOFF! READERS, AN IMPRINT OF BELLWETHER MEDIA BY FLUTTERBEE

Blastoff! Readers are carefully developed by literacy experts to build reading stamina and move students toward fluency by combining standards-based content with developmentally appropriate text.

Level 1 provides the most support through repetition of high-frequency words, light text, predictable sentence patterns, and strong visual support.

Level 2 offers early readers a bit more challenge through varied sentences, increased text load, and text-supportive special features.

Level 3 advances early-fluent readers toward fluency through increased text load, less reliance on photos, advancing concepts, longer sentences, and more complex special features.

★ **Blastoff! Universe**

Reading Level

Grade K

Grades 1–3

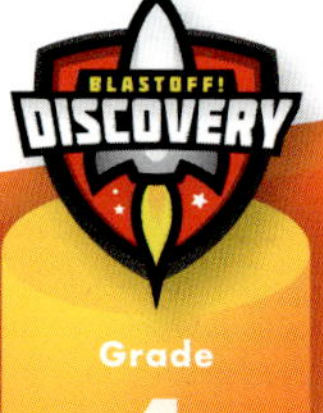

Grade 4

This edition first published in 2026 by Bellwether Media, Inc.

Text copyright © 2026 by Bellwether Media, Inc. All rights reserved. No part of this publication may be reproduced, stored in any retrieval system, or transmitted in any form or by any means, electronic, mechanical, photocopying, recording, or otherwise, without written permission of the publisher.

BLASTOFF! READERS and associated logos are trademarks and/or registered trademarks of Bellwether Media, Inc. Bellwether Media is a division of FlutterBee Education Group.

For information regarding permission, write to Bellwether Media, Inc., Attention: Permissions Department, 3500 American Blvd W, Suite 150, Bloomington, MN 55431.

Library of Congress Cataloging-in-Publication Data is available at www.loc.gov or upon request from the publisher.

ISBN: 9798893048049 (hardcover)
ISBN: 9798893049046 (ebook)

Editor: Betsy Rathburn   Designer: Laura Sowers

Table of Contents

What Is Angkor Wat?

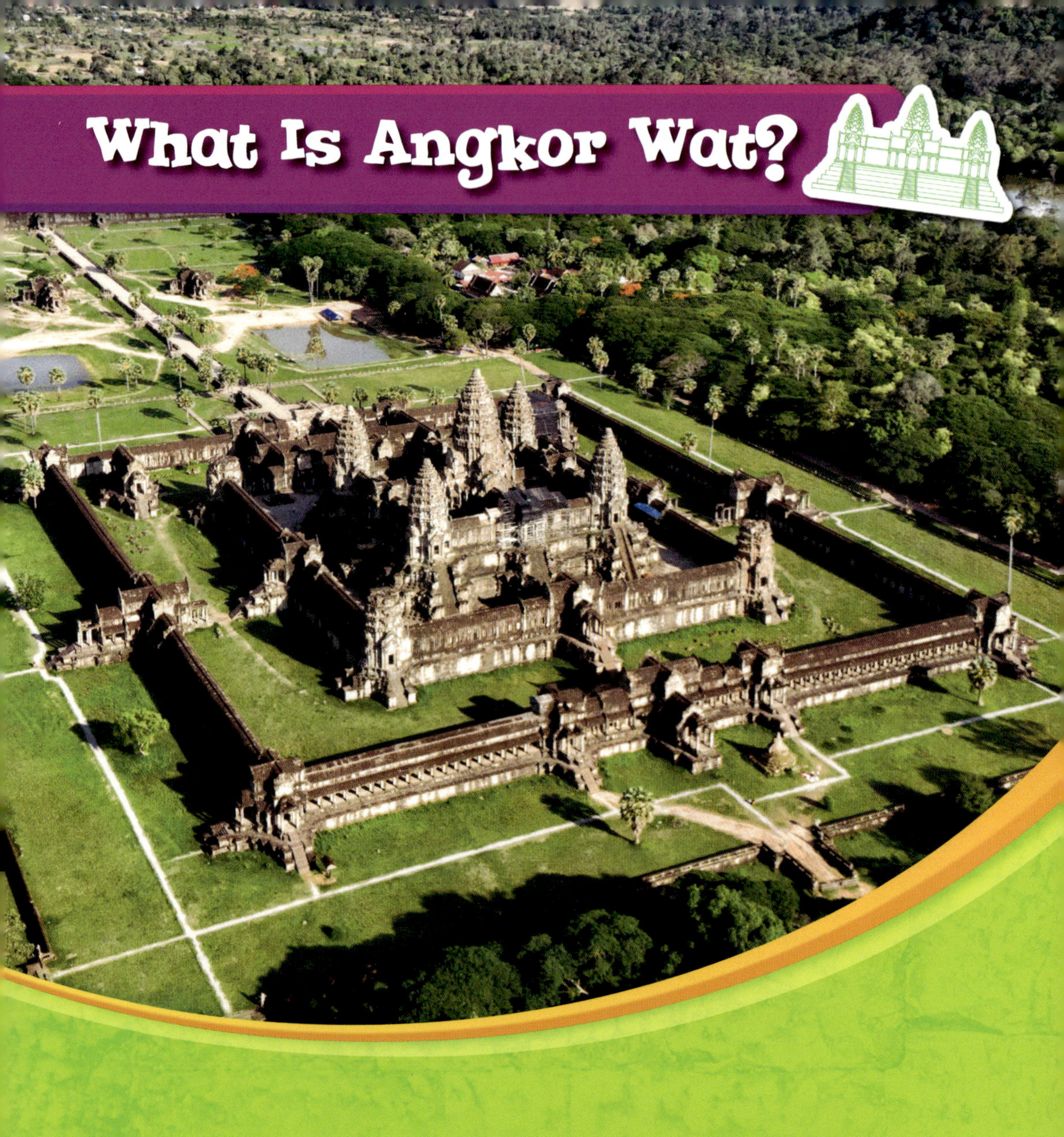

Angkor Wat is the world's biggest **religious** site. It is in the jungles of Cambodia. It has many temples.

Its name means
"city of temples."

Building Location

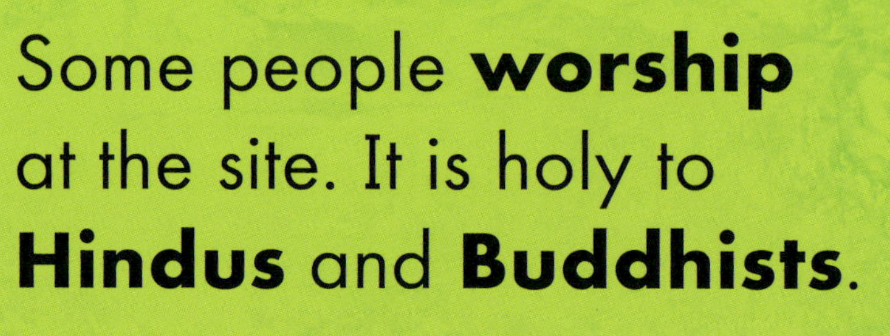

Some people **worship** at the site. It is holy to **Hindus** and **Buddhists**.

Buddhist praying at Angkor Wat

Tourists also visit. They see its **architecture**. They learn about its history.

History of Angkor Wat

King Suryavarman II

Angkor Wat was built in the 1100s. King Suryavarman II ordered it to be built.

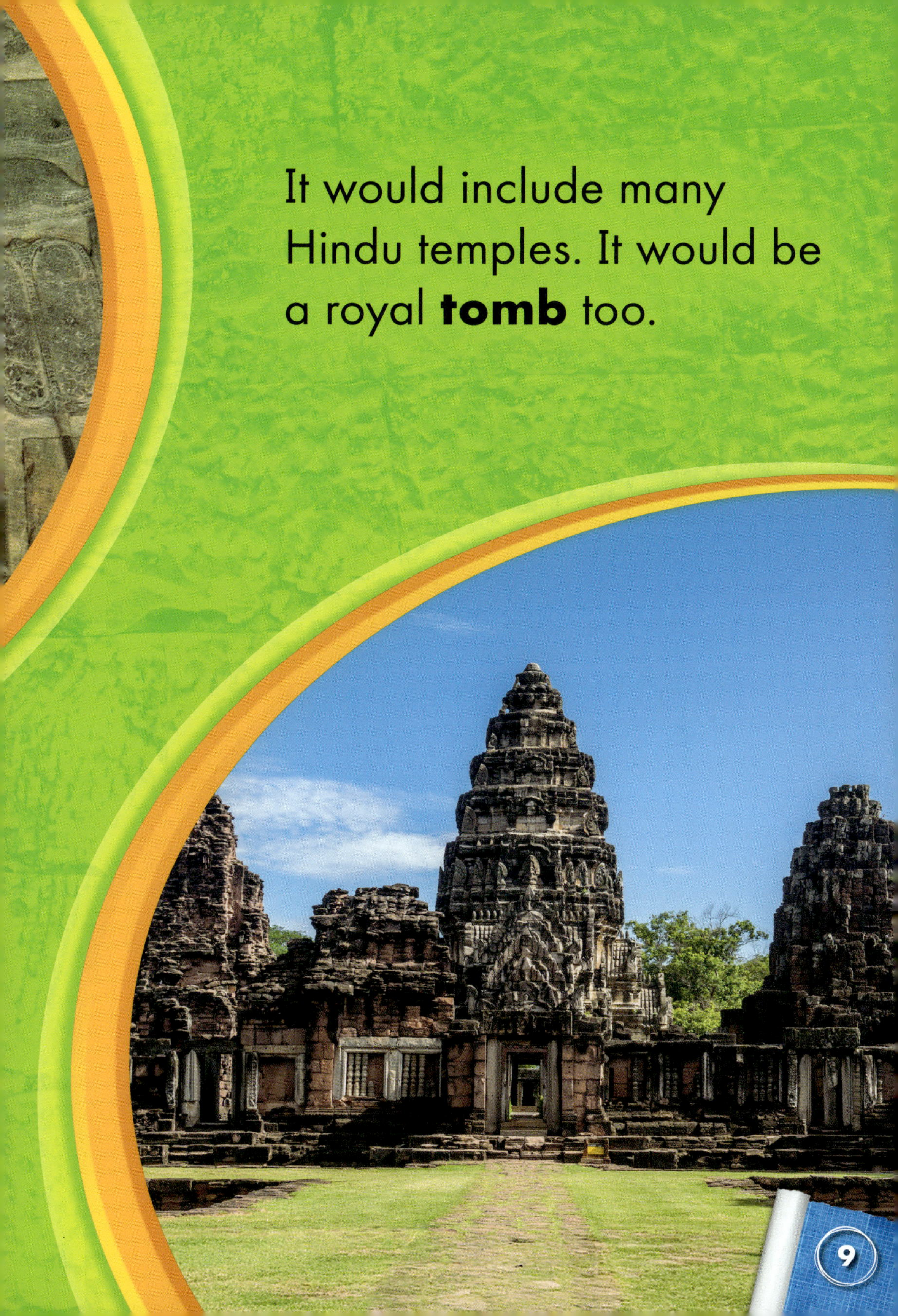

It would include many Hindu temples. It would be a royal **tomb** too.

The soil under the site was weak. Workers mixed water and sand. This made the soil stronger.

Workers built a **moat** around the site. It would provide more water. This would keep the **foundation** strong.

moat

A lot of stone was needed for building. Elephants helped move sandstone to the worksite. **Laterite** was used in many walls.

About 300,000 people worked on the project. It took around 37 years to finish.

Buddhists mainly used the site by the late 1100s. Buddhist statues replaced many Hindu ones.

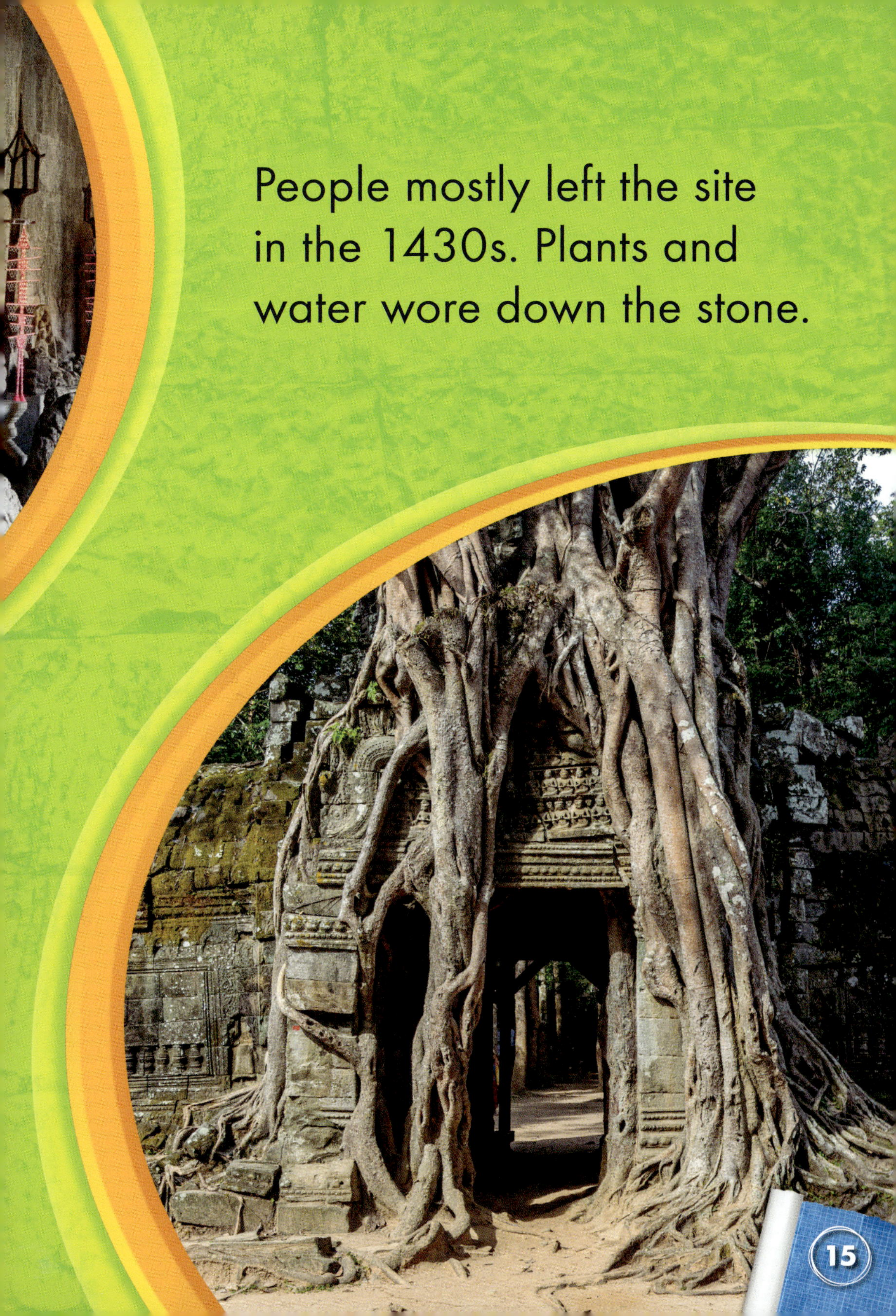

People mostly left the site in the 1430s. Plants and water wore down the stone.

Parts of Angkor Wat

Angkor Wat has over 1,000 buildings. It also has courtyards. It has **galleries** too.

Its **bas-reliefs** are famous. They tell many Hindu stories. They have Buddhist parts too.

bas-relief

Churning of the Ocean of Milk
What It Is
a bas-relief carving
What It Shows
a story about Hindu gods
gallery

The site's **design** shows parts of the Hindu **universe**. It has five towers. These stand for Mount Meru. This is a holy mountain.

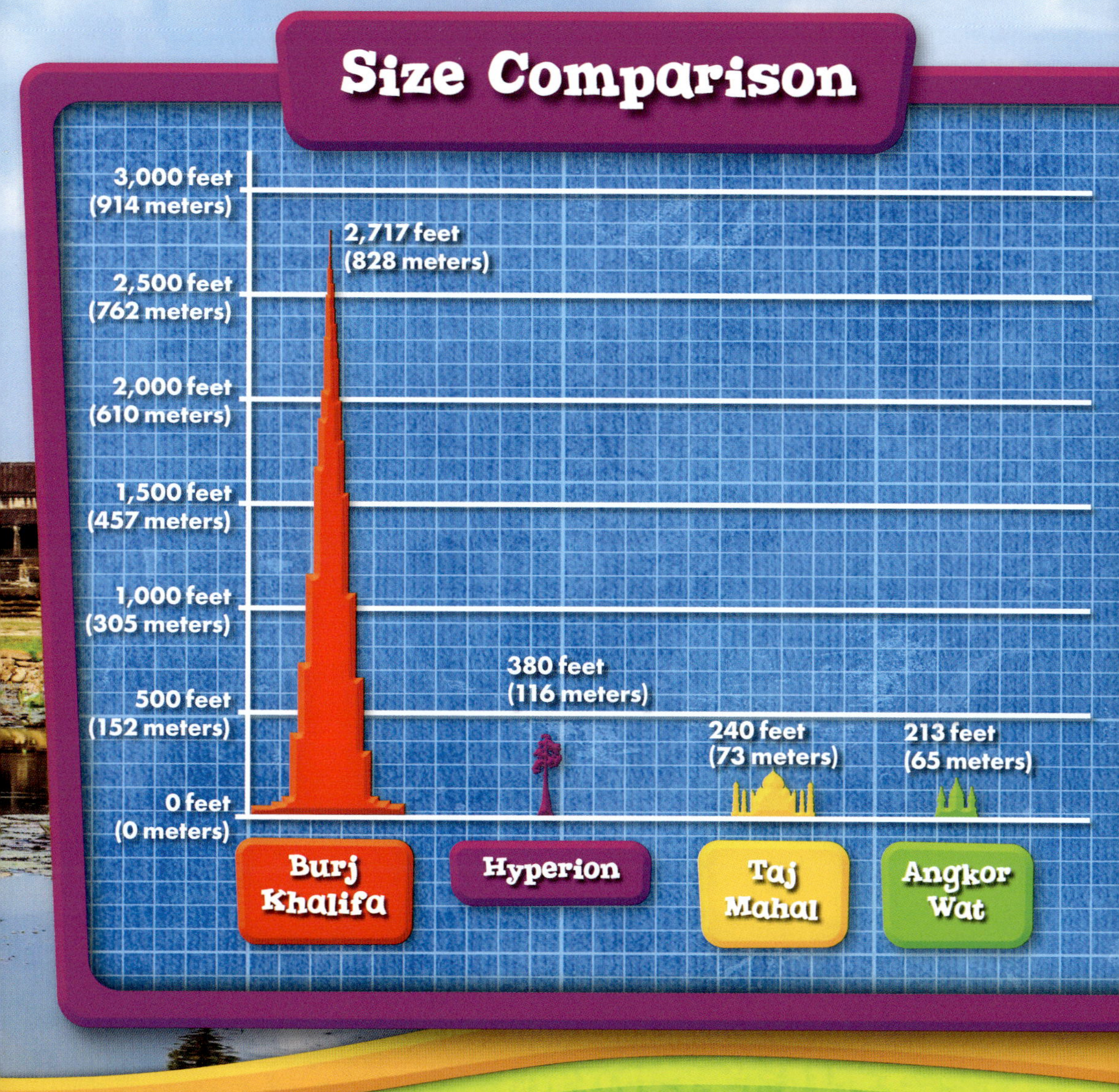

The outer walls stand for mountains. The moat stands for oceans beyond.

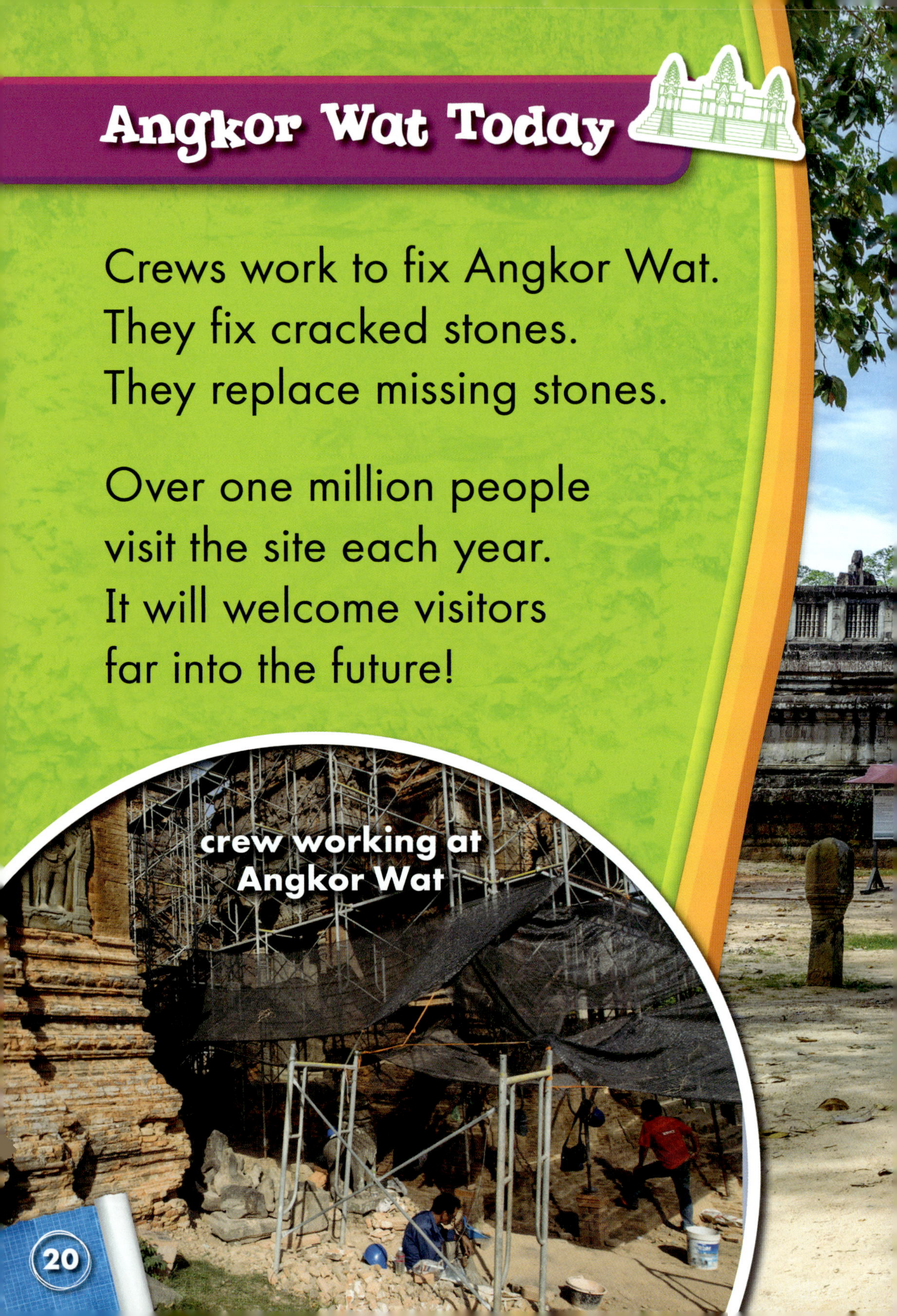

Angkor Wat Today

Crews work to fix Angkor Wat. They fix cracked stones. They replace missing stones.

Over one million people visit the site each year. It will welcome visitors far into the future!

crew working at Angkor Wat

Glossary

architecture—the design and structure of buildings

bas-reliefs—carvings where the art slightly stands out from the surrounding surface

Buddhists—followers of the religion Buddhism, based on the teachings of Buddha

design—a plan for a building, object, or pattern

foundation—the base or support on which a building rests

galleries—long, narrow passageways

Hindus—followers of Hinduism, a religion practiced in India and other parts of the world

laterite—a reddish clay soil that contains iron and aluminum

moat—a wide, deep trench around the wall of a large building that is usually filled with water

religious—having to do with a certain faith

tomb—a building used to house the dead

tourists—people who travel to visit another place

universe—all of space and everything in it, including planets, stars, and galaxies

worship—to show respect and love for a god

To Learn More

AT THE LIBRARY

Davies, Monika. *Cambodia.* Minneapolis, Minn.: Bellwether Media, 2024.

Ross, Melissa. *Angkor Wat.* Lake Elmo, Minn.: Focus Readers, 2023.

Spanier, Kristine. *Angkor Wat.* Minneapolis, Minn.: Jump!, 2022.

ON THE WEB

FACTSURFER

Factsurfer.com gives you a safe, fun way to find more information.

1. Go to www.factsurfer.com.

2. Enter "Angkor Wat" into the search box and click 🔍.

3. Select your book cover to see a list of related content.

Index

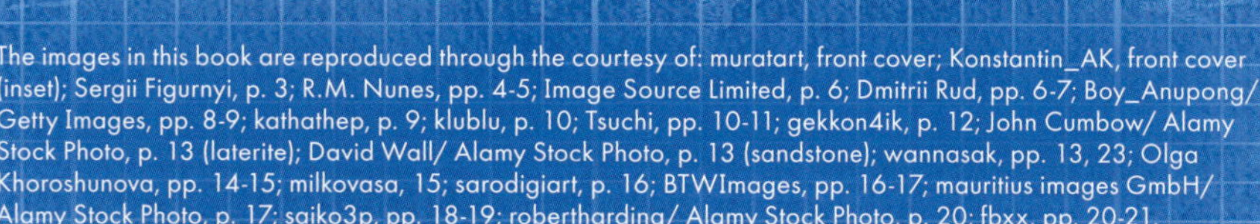

The images in this book are reproduced through the courtesy of: muratart, front cover; Konstantin_AK, front cover (inset); Sergii Figurnyi, p. 3; R.M. Nunes, pp. 4-5; Image Source Limited, p. 6; Dmitrii Rud, pp. 6-7; Boy_Anupong/ Getty Images, pp. 8-9; kathathep, p. 9; klublu, p. 10; Tsuchi, pp. 10-11; gekkon4ik, p. 12; John Cumbow/ Alamy Stock Photo, p. 13 (laterite); David Wall/ Alamy Stock Photo, p. 13 (sandstone); wannasak, pp. 13, 23; Olga Khoroshunova, pp. 14-15; milkovasa, 15; sarodigiart, p. 16; BTWImages, pp. 16-17; mauritius images GmbH/ Alamy Stock Photo, p. 17; saiko3p, pp. 18-19; robertharding/ Alamy Stock Photo, p. 20; fbxx, pp. 20-21.